YOUR KNOWLEDGE HAS VALUE

AF156256

- We will publish your bachelor's and
  master's thesis, essays and papers

- Your own eBook and book -
  sold worldwide in all relevant shops

- Earn money with each sale

Upload your text at www.GRIN.com
and publish for free

Klaus Würzer

The consequences of the attacks of 11, September

GRIN Verlag

Bibliografische Information der Deutschen Nationalbibliothek:

Die Deutsche Bibliothek verzeichnet diese Publikation in der Deutschen National-
bibliografie; detaillierte bibliografische Daten sind im Internet über http://dnb.d-
nb.de/ abrufbar.

Dieses Werk sowie alle darin enthaltenen einzelnen Beiträge und Abbildungen
sind urheberrechtlich geschützt. Jede Verwertung, die nicht ausdrücklich vom
Urheberrechtsschutz zugelassen ist, bedarf der vorherigen Zustimmung des Verla-
ges. Das gilt insbesondere für Vervielfältigungen, Bearbeitungen, Übersetzungen,
Mikroverfilmungen, Auswertungen durch Datenbanken und für die Einspeicherung
und Verarbeitung in elektronische Systeme. Alle Rechte, auch die des auszugsweisen
Nachdrucks, der fotomechanischen Wiedergabe (einschließlich Mikrokopie) sowie
der Auswertung durch Datenbanken oder ähnliche Einrichtungen, vorbehalten.

Imprint:

Copyright © 2013 GRIN Verlag GmbH
Druck und Bindung: Books on Demand GmbH, Norderstedt Germany
ISBN: 978-3-656-41789-7

This book at GRIN:

http://www.grin.com/en/e-book/213487/the-consequences-of-the-attacks-of-11-
september

GRIN - Your knowledge has value

Der GRIN Verlag publiziert seit 1998 wissenschaftliche Arbeiten von Studenten, Hochschullehrern und anderen Akademikern als eBook und gedrucktes Buch. Die Verlagswebsite www.grin.com ist die ideale Plattform zur Veröffentlichung von Hausarbeiten, Abschlussarbeiten, wissenschaftlichen Aufsätzen, Dissertationen und Fachbüchern.

Visit us on the internet:

http://www.grin.com/

http://www.facebook.com/grincom

http://www.twitter.com/grin_com

(school)

TERM PAPER IN

ADVANCED COURSE (ENGLISH)

(THE CONSEQUENCES OF THE ATTACKS OF 11,

SEPTEMBER)

Author:	(…)
The course instructor:	(…)
Processing time:	(…) Weeks
Deadline:	February the 13th, 2013

Structure/contents

1. Introduction

1.1 September 11, 2001 important facts

On September 11, 2001 a total of 19 terrorists hijacked 4 civilian aircraft and headed to different targets in the United States. Two planes were steered into the two towers of the World Trade Center in New York City, the third plane hit the pentagon in Arlington, Virginia the fourth plane which headed to the United States Capitol in Washington, D.C. crashed into a field near Shanksville, Pennsylvania. The two towers in New York City collapsed because of the large explosion that was caused by the large amount of fuel remaining in the aircraft. The collapse caused damage to the other buildings of the WTC so that some hours later the seventh of the building complex collapsed too. The attack in New York City killed 2,606 people inside the towers, the aircraft and on the ground. The third plane hit the west side of the Pentagon and killed 189 people. The crash of the plane in Arlington costs the life of all 44 passengers. A total of 2,996 people lost their life on the September 11 attacks including operational forces of the police and firefighters.[1]

1.2 Attackers and their background

The FBI published the names of all 19 hijackers two days after the attacks. The pilots of the plains who attacked the WTC were Mohammed Atta and Marwan al-Shehhi. The plain which hit the pentagon was controlled by Hani Hanjour. The machine that crashed on the ground in Shanksville was flown by Ziad Jarrah. All hijackers were born in Arab countries and belonged to the same group of radical Islamists.[2]

Mohamed Atta was born on September 1, 1968 in Kafr el-Sheikh, Egypt. He grew up in Cairo and made a study of architecture which he graduated with a diploma. Afterwards he moved to Germany and studied urban planning at the Technical University of Hamburg Harburg. From 1998 to 2001 he lived together with Ramzi Binalshibh and Said Bahaji who are members of the "Hamburg cell". Mohamed and his roommates were members of the Salafist branch of the Islam.[3]

1/2   SpiegelTV DVD 11. September

3   http://en.wikipedia.org/wiki/September_11_attacks

Marwan al-Shehhi was born on May 9, 1978 in the United Arab Emirates. In 1999 he moved to Hamburg and set up the Hamburg cell together with Mohamed Atta and Ramzi Binalshibh. At the end of 1999, Marwan traveled to Afghanistan to meet members of the al-Qaida terror organization. In March 2000 he went back to Germany. 2 month later Marwan flew to the US and acquired a pilot's license in Venice, Florida. [4]

Hani Hanjour was born on August 13, 1972 in Ta'if, Saudi Arabia. In contrast to the other terrorists he already lived many years in the U.S. before the attacks on September 11. He frequently met with the terrorists who committed the attacks with him later. Hani successfully completed a flight training in Tucson, Arizona. He remained in America although he could not find work because of his bad English knowledge.[5]

Ziad Jarrah was born on May 11, 1975 in Mazraa, Lebanon. He moved to Germany in 1996 where he starts to study at the Technical University of Hamburg Harburg together with Mohamed Atta and other Islamists who were also involved in the attacks later. Ziad belongs to the Hamburg cell and was involved in the planning of the 9/11 attacks.[6]

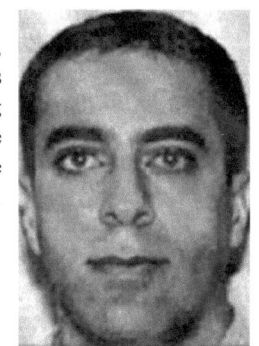

4/5/6 http://en.wikipedia.org/wiki/September_11_attacks

The Hamburg cell was the designation of a group whose members were responsible for the planning and the implementation of the 9/11 attacks. The group was in close contact to al-Qaeda and Osama bin Laden. 3 of 4 terrorists who flew the 4 planes were members of the cell and met regularly in Mohammed Atta's apartment in Hamburg-Eißendorf. The exact number of members is unknown but it is clear that the group consisted of at least 7 people. The members who were not involved in the implementation of the attacks fled from Germany in order to avoid being arrested for the planning. The terrorists goal was to defend the religious intention of their radical Islamic believes to kill unbelieving people and to form a new world a world with Islamic values.[7]

1.3 Why did I choose this topic

I have to confess that the events of September 11th have never left me. When I saw the news on that day I was surprised how something like this could happen to such a powerful nation like the United States of America and what would happen next. In the following years the picture of two burning towers of the World Trade Center burned into my memory. I always tried to understand the intentions of the al-Qaeda terrorists and why the war in Afghanistan started. A war in which many western nations including Germany are involved to protect the own population against radical Islamists. Today I know that the war was necessary to save many lives and to preserve the face of America. Nevertheless people raise doubts on the official reason for the Afghanistan war which was the fight against terrorism. People saw the poor sales of the gun lobby and wondered if it was just coincidence that the attacks happened in exactly the time when the gun lobby had problems to find enough buyers for their firearms or if it was a plan of the U.S. government to boost the economy. More than 11 years after the attacks there are dozens of theories of what happened on the day of 9/11. It is fact that terrorists committed the attacks and they were members of the al-Qaeda terror organization. There are no evidences for a connection of the government in this incident. It would be hard to imagine that the U.S. government kills people to help companies earning more money. In my work I want to clarify the correlations between the attacks and the resulting consequences. Therefore I start with the official declaration of the government about 9/11.

2. President Bush's speech after 9/11

2.1 Meaning and content

On the evening of September 20, 2001 President Georg W. Bush held a speech to the American Nation and the whole world. The world was waiting for the President's statement about the attacks a week ago. The speech starts with an enumeration of the wars that American people have experienced and the note that all previous wars took place on foreign soils. He emphasizes the attack on American soil in contrast to the

7 http://en.wikipedia.org/wiki/Hamburg_cell

other wars in which the U.S. was involved. Bush explained to the audience who committed the attacks and refers to the terror organization al-Qaeda as those responsible

responsible. The goal of the terrorists is to organize the world new. In his further explanations he mentioned Osama bin Laden as the leader of al-Qaeda and the brutal methods of the Taliban regime in Afghanistan and more than 60 other countries. The President particularly emphasizes the questionable views of the Taliban such as the prohibition of televisions and the prohibition of short beards for male Muslims. Bush nevertheless indicates that the American people respect the Afghan population and mentioned the help of his country that the Afghans receive. Furthermore, the delivery of the terrorists to the United States, the protection of foreign persons and the closure of the al-Qaeda training camps is demanded in the speech. All previous content is working towards the climax of the speech. This climax is the war against terrorism or better known as ''War on Terror''. The President announces that the United States will use any possibility to fight against terrorism in the world with the military but also with closing of bank accounts to stop the funding of al-Qaeda training camps and other terrorist facilities. Bush asks the other nations of the world to do the same and to support the United States in this global fight against terrorism. The speech can be seen as a preparation of the then President Georg W. Bush for the American Nation in view of the following war in Afghanistan and the limitations in the lives of Americans. The President tries to explain to the citizens why so many people had to die and how the Nation will react to those attacks in the following time. In the knowledge that many other people on the world watch his speech live on television Bush tries to show strength and endurance. Among the Spectators are also the responsible persons for the attacks such as Osama bin Laden who are waiting for signs of weakness of the President in an exceptional situation like this. About the appearance of the President can be noted that he was under very high pressure after the attacks and still had to make the appearance of serenity.[8]

The speech acts like a declaration of war to all countries of the world which are not on the side of America. Countries which do not want to get involved in a war between Western Nations and Muslim countries are presented as enemies of the U.S. The President shows this view about the forthcoming war in Afghanistan clearly and leaves the allied states hardly any freedom of decision. Either they fight on the side of America or they are considered as enemies.

2.2 Relation to the American Dream

Considering the far-reaching consequences of the new security policy in the U.S. many people's desire for freedom became awake. This desire is firmly anchored in the memories of most Americans and is also known as the "American Dream" many settlers who immigrated to America searched for religious freedom but also for freedom of expression and independence. These were the reasons why people came to America and they fought hard against the British troops to defend their new rights. After President

---

8 http://www.youtube.com/watch?v=mP-b9J4OFhU

Bush's speech many people saw their rights threatened and President Bush who was already criticized for his approach in other countries became more unpopular in the United States. Despite all the criticism Bush continues the fight against terrorism and the fight for freedom.

3. Aftermath

3.1 "War on Terror"

"War on Terror" was the official designation of the U.S. government for the international fight against terrorism. This description includes not only military steps, but also legal measures. The 40th United States President Ronald Reagan used this name for the first time in 1985 supplied in the attacks on international peacekeepers in Beirut and other attacks in the year before. The spread of the name however took place by George W. Bush the 43th U.S. President after the attacks on September 11, 2001. This was an announcement for a global war against terrorism.

In October 2001 the U.S. government published a list of the 22 most wanted terrorists. In the same month British and American military forces started the hunt for terrorists on the East African coast. On October 26, 2001 the "Patriot Act" becomes legally in the U.S. This law is used to support the hunt for terrorist and the protection of American citizens. In threats the fundamental rights of the population can be restricted. The Patriot Act facilitates especially the work of the FBI, which is the competent authority when it comes to cases of internal security. A typical approach in those cases is the phone and internet surveillance without the necessity of a judicial authorization. Also house searchings may take place without the knowledge of the owner. Basically, the authorities have the right to monitor any citizen of the United States even if no evidence is available against a person. In addition the act expands the task area of the American Foreign Intelligence known as the CIA. The authority got the permission to determine in their own country. For non-Americans which travel to the USA, it means that their private data such as the flight booking hotel booking and car rental booking will be recorded and retained for a certain period. Those who have already been to the U.S. know the cards that must be filled with personal data such as the travel destination and the length of the stay. In Europe and other countries, such cuts of fundamental rights would be simply inconceivable. Nevertheless, there are also measures in Germany to curb international terrorism. A database to ensure data of terror suspects in German "Antiterrordatei" is conducted by various authorities. The database has the purpose to track suspicious people by recording internet activities and telephone calls. Furthermore, the possession of weapons and the religious affiliation is being noted. In 2011 the number of all registered persons was 18,280. [9]

---

9 http://en.wikipedia.org/wiki/War_on_Terror

3.2 The view on Muslim after the terroristic attacks

Even if the War on Terror was the most significant consequence of the destruction of American property there were also side effects. The hate on Muslim is widespread in Christian countries today. Western people often associate Islam with terrorism this is illustrated by the fact that the first thought of many people if they think about Islam is al-Qaeda and the 9/11 attacks. That is not correct because the Quran forbids Muslim to

kill people. Nevertheless there are passages in the Quran where murder is not clearly identified as a criminal offense. Radical groups like al-Qaeda see this as a call to kill people who are not Muslims. They fight in strong faith to build an Islamic super state without consideration for losses. The opponents of Islam disregard that many Muslims died in the attacks too and Muslims belong to the American society as Jews and Christians. There is no reason to despise Muslims when fringe groups like the Taliban want to spread their radical ideas because there are also marginalized groups in Christianity, Hinduism and Judaism. There are terrorists in all religions and they don't need to have a religious background.

Generally the hate on Muslims can be summarized under the name Islamophobia. The origins of this name lie back in the middle ages. In those days there were almost only Christians in Europe and the view on Muslim was negative through and through which meant that people from other Religions were persecuted. The reason for the behavior of Christians is that they see their own way of life as the best way of life. Other religions such as the Islam have different values and that makes it different to understand the way people live in a different religion. The familiar is considered accurate and the unknown is considered disruptive.

Nowadays Muslims are seen very differently on the world. Who has dealt with the Muslim faith knows that Islam is a religion in which much is based on respect and in no way intends to inflict harm on people of other religions. Who, mainly come into contact

with the negative religion probably Muslims. On anti- over Europe and the show cartoons which Perhaps the best Westergaard. He was Døstrup, Denmark. Muhammad cartoons illustration of a bomb on his head aspects of the not very old misinterprets the faith of Islamic demonstrations all U.S. opponents of Islam make Islam ridiculous. known cartoonist is Kurt born on July 13, 1935 in He published twelve including the well-known Prophet Muhammad with instead of a turban.

10

---

10 http://europenews.dk/files/Jeden-Tag-eine-Mohammed-Karikatur.png

The cartoon shows a Muslim, more specifically Prophet Muhammad. He wears a beard which is typical for male Muslims. On his head he wears a bomb with a burning fuse. On the bomb are some Arabic graphic characters which stand for an Islamic creed. Muhammad glimpse is strictly directed forward and his face radiates hate or anger. The consequences of the publication of this picture were far reaching and the society split into two groups. In one group were the proponents of freedom of expression and the other group consisted mainly of supporters of Muslims and people who wanted to prevent that people were harmed in clashes between Muslims and right-wing people. During clashes in several countries which were caused by Westergaard's cartoon more than 50 people died. Several murderous attacks on Kurt Westergaard were prevented by the Danish police. The cartoonist and his wife are currently under police protection and they will be for many more years. Westergaard sees himself as an advocate of freedom of expression and does not want his cartoon used by right-wing politics such as Pro NRW an Anti-Islam party in North Rhine-Westphalia the most populous state in Germany. However he can poorly prevent that his cartoons will be used to provoke Muslims in the future. For his fearless advocacy for freedom of expression Westergaard received one freedom Award which was presented by the German Chancellor Angela Merkel in Potsdam and a second Award for media freedom in Leipzig. Several former winners protested against the award but could not prevent the transfer.

3.3 Change of the American national consciousness

Not just the perception of Islam has changed with the Americans also the strong confidence of the American people has been questioned. After 9/11 the strong superpower was no longer unassailable and Americans had to see that their values were not wanted at all places in the world. Many wondered why people were so angry about America that they perpetrate attacks on a Nation that brings peace and justice to all countries which possess no democracy. Slowly it became clear that America has charged a lot of hate over the last decades outside of Europe in states with non-Western values. The Middle East and particularly countries in which US troops invaded after 9/11 had leaders that were the greatest adversary of the United States. Despite all doubts about the power of their own Nation, America was still the greatest military power on the world and could launch attacks at any time which was possible because heavily armed combat ships were in every ocean at that time and still are today. The national consciousness of the Americans today is unabated. The flag is shown with pride but they know that in times of nuclear rockets there can be a new attack at any time.

4. Formulation of a result

4.1 My own opinion about what happened after September 11 attacks

In my opinion the attacks of September 11 were at large parts personal negligence of the United States. The many wars for freedom and equal rights and the constant presence of US troops in crisis countries have fueled a real hatred for America and its citizens. Indeed were the attacks on 9/11 exaggerated and less predictable nevertheless an attack was not ruled out. The self-confidence of American citizens almost requires

a setback. It is important to use the military power carefully and not to deter or intimidate other nations. Americans have learned the hard way what it means to defend their rights. Rights for which they have fought in the American independence war in the 18th century and now want to give these rights to all people around the world. The war in Afghanistan cost many lives. Not only American and European soldiers were killed but also thousands of civilians, often children by a war that is inevitable. Many people say it was a mistake to send German troops to Afghanistan to support the American army but they forget that Americans gave us Germans freedom and independence after Hitler led war against the whole world. Our democracy today is based on American values and we are grateful to them. Now people will say that we paid our debt back and we have to move because all this happened nearly 70 years ago. That's right but don't we have the obligation to save people's lives which are in danger when Taliban groups like al-Qaeda dictate people how they should live and dissenting people are killed? Don't we have the duty to spread our democracy, rights and freedom? Everyone should have the same rights on earth independent of race and religion. I think people forget how well our society in the West is and how bad it is other countries. We Germans cannot close our eyes to the truth that terroristic attacks can happen at any time in our country. The hatred of the Taliban is not just on America it is on all Western countries. We should not wait for an attack in Germany we should react before this happens. In my opinion the use of German soldiers in Afghanistan is justified, as a fight for freedom and equality that benefits us all.

5. Sources

1.1 DVD: 11. September – SpiegelTV Hamburg 2006

1.2 Mohamed Atta: http://en.wikipedia.org/wiki/Mohamed_Atta
(used on January 29, 2013)

    Marwan al-Shehhi: http://en.wikipedia.org/wiki/Marwan_al-Shehhi
(used on January 29, 2013)

    Hani Hanjour: http://en.wikipedia.org/wiki/Hani_Hanjour
(used on January 29, 2013)

    Ziad Jarrah: http://en.wikipedia.org/wiki/Ziad_Jarrah
(used on January 29, 2013)

All pictures of the terrorists are taken from the respective website

2.1 YouTube Movie: http://www.youtube.com/watch?v=mP-b9J4OFhU

2.1   http://en.wikipedia.org/wiki/War_on_Terror

2.2 Cartoon: http://europenews.dk/files/Jeden-Tag-eine-Mohammed-Karikatur.png